REVISED EDITION

Plannin for Learning through Journeys

by Judith Harries Illustrated by Cathy Hughes

Contents

Published by Step Forward Publishing Limited

St Jude's Church, Dulwich Road, Herne Hill, London, SE24 0PB Tel. 020 7738 5454

Revised edition © Step Forward Publishing Limited 2008

First edition © Step Forward Publishing Limited 2007

www.practicalpreschoolbooks.com

Planning for Learning through Journeys ISBN: 978 1 90457 559 7

Making plans

Why plan?

The purpose of planning is to make sure that all children enjoy a broad and balanced curriculum. All planning should be useful. Plans are working documents that you spend time preparing, but which should later repay your efforts. Try to be concise. This will help you in finding information quickly when you need it.

Long-term plans

Preparing a long-term plan, which maps out the curriculum during a year or even two, will help you to ensure that you are providing a variety of activities and are meeting the statutory requirements of the *Statutory Framework for the Early Years Foundation Stage: Setting the Standards for Learning, Development and Care for Children from Birth to Five: Every Child Matters* (2007).

Your long-term plan need not be detailed. Divide the time period over which you are planning into fairly equal sections, such as half terms. Choose a topic for each section. Young children benefit from making links between the new ideas they encounter so as you select each topic, think about the time of year in which you plan to do it. A topic about minibeasts will not be very successful in November!

Although each topic will address all the learning areas, some could focus on a specific area. For example, a topic

on Journeys would lend itself well to activities relating to Knowledge and Understanding of the World and Physical Development. Another topic might particularly encourage the appreciation of stories. Try to make sure that you provide a variety of topics in your long-term plans.

Autumn 1	Nursery rhymes
Autumn 2	Food/Christmas
Spring 1	People who help us
Spring 2	Animals
Summer 1	Clothes
Summer 2	Journeys

Medium-term plans

Medium-term plans will outline the contents of a topic in a little more detail. One way to start this process is by brainstorming on a large piece of paper. Work with your team writing down all the activities you can think of which are relevant to the topic. As you do this it may become clear that some activities go well together. Think about dividing them into themes. The topic of Journeys, for example, has themes such as 'On foot', 'By road', 'On or under water', and 'Through the air'. At this stage it is helpful to make a chart. Write the theme ideas down the side of the chart and put a different area of learning at the top of each column. Now you can insert your brainstormed ideas and will quickly see where there are gaps. As you complete the chart take account of children's earlier experiences and provide opportunities for them to progress.

Refer back to *The Early Years Foundation Stage* document and check that you have addressed as many different aspects of it as you can. Once all your medium-term plans are complete make sure that there are no neglected areas.

Day-to-day plans

The plans you make for each day will outline aspects such as:

- resources needed;
- the way in which you might introduce activities;
- individual needs;
- the organisation of adult help;

Making plans

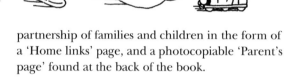

- size of the group;
- safety;
- timing;
- key vocabulary.

Identify the learning and the ELGs that each activity is intended to promote. Make a note of any assessments or observations that you are likely to carry out. On your plans make notes of activities that were particularly successful, or any changes you would make another time.

A final note

Planning should be seen as flexible. Not all groups meet every day, and not all children attend every day. Any part of the plan can be used independently, stretched over a longer period or condensed to meet the needs of any group. You will almost certainly adapt the activities as children respond to them in different ways and bring their own ideas, interests and enthusiasms. The important thing is to ensure that the children are provided with a varied and enjoyable curriculum that meets their individual developing needs.

Using the book

- Collect or prepare suggested resources as listed on page 21.
- Read the section which outlines links to the Early Learning Goals (pages 4-7) and explains the rationale for the topic of Journeys.
- For each weekly theme two activities are described in detail as an example to help you in your planning and preparation. Key vocabulary, questions and learning opportunities are identified.
- The skills chart on page 23 will help you to see at a glance which aspects of children's development are being addressed as a focus each week.
- As children take part in the Journeys topic activities, their learning will progress. 'Collecting evidence' on page 22 explains how you might monitor children's achievements.
- Find out on page 20 how the topic can be brought together in a grand outing involving parents, children and friends.
- There is additional material to support the working

partnership of families and children in the form of a 'Home links' page, and a photocopiable 'Parent's page' found at the back of the book.

It is important to appreciate that the ideas presented in this book will only be a part of your planning. Many activities that will be taking place as routine in your group may not be mentioned. For example, it is assumed that sand, dough, water, puzzles, floor toys and large scale apparatus are part of the ongoing pre-school experience, as are the opportunities which increasing numbers of groups are able to offer for children to develop ICT skills. Role-play areas, stories, rhymes and singing, and group discussion times are similarly assumed to be happening each week although they may not be a focus for described activities.

Using this book in Northern Ireland, Scotland and Wales

Although the curriculum guidelines in Northern Ireland, Scotland and Wales differ, the activities in this book are still appropriate for use throughout the United Kingdom. They are designed to promote the development of early skills and to represent good practice in the early years

Glossary

EYFS: Early Years Foundation Stage
ELG: Early Learning Goal

Using the 'Early Learning Goals'

Having chosen your topic and made your medium- term plans you can use the *Statutory Framework for the Early Years Foundation Stage* document to highlight the key learning opportunities your activities will address. The Early Learning Goals are split into six areas: Personal, Social and Emotional Development; Communication, Language and Literacy; Problem Solving, Reasoning and Numeracy; Knowledge and Understanding of the World; Physical Development and Creative Development. Do not expect each of your topics to cover every goal but your long-term plans should allow for all of them to be addressed by the time a child enters Year 1.

The following section highlights parts of the Statutory Framework in point form to show what children are expected to be able to do in each area of learning by the time they enter Year 1. These points will be used throughout this book to show how activities for a topic on Journeys link to these expectations. For example, Personal, Social and Emotional Development point 7 is 'form good relationships with adults and peers'. Activities suggested which provide the opportunity for children to do this will have the reference PS7. This will enable you to see which parts of the Early Learning Goals are covered in a given week and plan for areas to be revisited and developed.

In addition, you can ensure that activities offer variety in the goals to be encountered. Often a similar activity may be carried out to achieve different learning objectives. For example, when going on a walk outside to look for animal tracks and trails, children will be developing aspects of Knowledge and Understanding of the World. They will also be learning to use personal and social skills as they work together as a group and explore new learning, and creative skills when they create pictures of snail trails.

Personal, Social and Emotional Development (PS)

This area of learning covers important aspects of development that affect the way children learn, behave and relate to others.

By the end of the Early Years Foundation Stage, children should:

PS1 Continue to be interested, excited and motivated to learn.

PS2 Be confident to try new activities, initiate ideas and speak in a familiar group.

PS3 Maintain attention, concentrate and sit quietly when appropriate.

PS4 Respond to significant experiences, showing a range of feelings when appropriate.

PS5 Have a developing awareness of their own needs, views and feelings and be sensitive to the needs, views and feelings of others.

PS6 Have a developing respect for their own cultures and beliefs and those of other people.

PS7 Form good relationships with adults and peers.

PS8 Work as part of a group or class, taking turns and sharing fairly, understanding that there needs to be agreed values and codes of behaviour for groups of people, including adults and children, to work together harmoniously.

PS9 Understand what is right, what is wrong and why.

PS10 Consider the consequences of their words and actions for themselves and others.

PS11 Dress and undress independently and manage their own personal hygiene.

PS12 Select and use activities and resources independently.

PS13 Understand that people have different needs, views, cultures and beliefs, that need to be treated with respect.

PS14 Understand that they can expect others to treat their needs, views, cultures and beliefs with respect.

The topic of Journeys provides valuable opportunities for children to develop awareness of the need to keep themselves and others safe. Time spent discussing different ways of travelling will encourage children to speak in a group, to share their feelings and to consider consequences. By playing circle games children will learn to take turns. Many of the areas outlined above will also be covered as children carry out the activities in other key areas. For example, when children play physical games and join in number rhymes they will also have the opportunity to develop PS8.

Communication, Language and Literacy (L)

By the end of the Early Years Foundation Stage, children should:

L1   Interact with others, negotiating plans and activities and taking turns in conversation.

L2   Enjoy listening to and using spoken and written language, and readily turn to it in their play and learning.

L3   Sustain attentive listening, responding to what they have heard with relevant comments, questions or actions.

L4   Listen with enjoyment, and respond to stories, songs and other music, rhymes and poems and make up their own stories, songs, rhymes and poems.

L5   Extend their vocabulary, exploring the meaning and sounds of new words.

L6   Speak clearly and audibly with confidence and control and show awareness of the listener.

L7   Use language to imagine and recreate roles and experiences.

L8   Use talk to organise, sequence and clarify thinking, ideas, feelings and events.

L9   Hear and say initial and final sounds in the order in which they occur.

L10   Link sounds to letters, naming and sounding the letters of the alphabet.

L11   Use their phonic knowledge to write simple regular words and make phonetically plausible attempts at more complex words.

L12   Explore and experiment with sounds, words and texts.

L13   Retell narratives in the correct sequence, drawing on language patterns of stories.

L14   Read a range of familiar and common words and simple sentences independently.

L15   Know that print carries meaning and in English is read from left to right and top to bottom.

L16   Show an understanding of the elements of stories, such as main character, sequence of events, and openings, and how information can be found in non-fiction texts to answer questions about where, who, why and how.

L17   Attempt writing for different purposes, using features of different forms such as lists, stories and instructions.

L18   Write their own names and other things such as labels and captions, and begin to form simple sentences, sometimes using punctuation.

L19   Use a pencil and hold it effectively to form recognisable letters, most of which are correctly formed.

The activities suggested for the theme of Journeys include several opportunities for the children to respond to well-known picture books and stories, using drama, and reinforcing and extending their vocabulary. Role-play areas are described that will allow children to use their imaginations as they plan their journeys at the travel agents and travel in different ways. Making passports will help children to develop their early writing skills. Throughout the topic, opportunities are given for children to explore the sounds of words and see some of their ideas recorded in both pictures and words.

Problem Solving, Reasoning and Numeracy (N)

By the end of the Early Years Foundation Stage, children should:

N1 Say and use number names in order in familiar contexts.

N2 Count reliably up to ten everyday objects.

N3 Recognise numerals 1 to 9.

N4 Use developing mathematical ideas and methods to solve practical problems.

N5 In practical activities and discussion, begin to use the vocabulary involved in adding and subtracting.

N6 Use language such as 'more' or 'less' to compare two numbers.

N7 Find one more or one less than a number from one to ten.

N8 Begin to relate addition to combining two groups of objects and subtraction to 'taking away'.

N9 Use language such as 'greater', 'smaller', 'heavier' or 'lighter' to compare quantities.

N10 Talk about, recognise and recreate simple patterns.

N11 Use language such as 'circle' or 'bigger' to describe the shape and size of solids and flat shapes.

N12 Use everyday words to describe position.

As children carry out the activities in this topic, they will develop mathematical skills in a meaningful context. Sorting and counting skills are used to compile a bar chart and put animals and vehicles into sets. Simple activities, such as timing journeys around the equipment introduce the concept of measuring time and distance. There are also opportunities for children to recognise numbers and shapes on road signs and use counting rhymes. Ordering suitcases by size and weight provides an opportunity for using mathematical language.

Knowledge and Understanding of the World (K)

By the end of the Early Years Foundation Stage, children should:

K1 Investigate objects and materials by using all of their senses as appropriate.

K2 Find out about, and identify, some features of living things, objects and events they observe.

K3 Look closely at similarities, differences, patterns and change.

K4 Ask questions about why things happen and how things work.

K5 Build and construct with a wide range of objects, selecting appropriate resources and adapting their work where necessary.

K6 Select the tools and techniques they need to shape, assemble and join materials they are using.

K7 Find out about and identify the uses of everyday technology and use information and communication technology and programmable toys to support their learning.

K8 Find out about past and present events in their own lives, and in those of their families and other people they know.

K9 Observe, find out about and identify features in the place they live and the natural world.

K10 Find out about their environment, and talk about those features they like and dislike.

K11 Begin to know about their own cultures and beliefs and those of other people.

The topic of Journeys provides many opportunities for children to find out about the place in which they live and the natural world as well as further afield. There are several activities which focus on designing and constructing vehicles using a variety of materials and tools. As they compare journeys past and present the children will look at similarities and differences. Throughout all activities children should be given the chance to talk about their experiences and to ask questions.

Physical Development (PD)

By the end of the Early Years Foundation Stage, children should:

PD1   Move with confidence, imagination and in safety.
PD2   Move with control and coordination.
PD3   Travel around, under, over and through balancing and climbing equipment.
PD4   Show awareness of space, of themselves and of others.
PD5   Recognise the importance of keeping healthy, and those things which contribute to this.
PD6   Recognise the changes that happen to their bodies when they are active.
PD7   use a range of small and large equipment
PD8   handle tools, objects, construction and malleable materials safely and with increasing control

Activities such as playing with balloons, riding sit-and-ride toys around a circuit, and following animal trails through tunnels and over balance beams will offer experience with a range of equipment. Several collaborative games offer opportunities to move with control, coordination, imagination and showing awareness of space.

Creative Development (C)

By the end of the Early Years Foundation Stage, children should:

C1   Respond in a variety of ways to what they see, hear, smell, touch and feel.
C2   Express and communicate their ideas, thoughts and feelings by using a widening range of materials, suitable tools, imaginative and role play, movement, designing and making, and a variety of songs and musical instruments.
C3   Explore colour, texture, shape, form and space in two or three dimensions.
C4   Recognise and explore how sounds can be changed, sing simple songs from memory, recognise repeated sounds and sound patterns and match movements to music.
C5   Use their imagination in art and design, music, dance, imaginative and role play and stories.

During this topic children will experience working with a variety of materials as they make model hot-air balloons, and salt-dough trains. Simple musical activities give opportunities for children to explore sounds and sing songs. They will print with their feet, wheels, and toy vehicles and express their ideas through a variety of media including paint, bubbles, collage and musical instruments.

Week 1
On foot

Personal, Social and Emotional Development

● Start the topic by taking the children on a 'journey on foot' around the area. Before you go out, talk about the need to hold hands, listen and stay together. Take photographs to use in later activities. Look at enlarged photographs of local places that the children may walk to such as the park, shops, library. Do they enjoy walking or do they prefer to go by car? (PS2, 3, 5)

● During circle time, talk about how it might feel to not be able to walk. Borrow some child-sized crutches or a wheelchair. How easy is it to get round the room in a wheelchair? (PS5, 13)

Communication, Language and Literacy

● Make a class book of 'Journeys the children have made ...', beginning this week with 'on foot' and add to it throughout the topic. Ask children to draw pictures of themselves on a favourite walk. Help them to write or scribe descriptions of what they might see. (L7, 8, 17)

● Read *Alfie's Feet* by Shirley Hughes (Red Fox). How did Alfie learn about left and right? Help the children to make left and right bracelets with L and R clearly marked. Can they tell you which hand they hold their pencil in? (L4, 10)

Problem Solving, Reasoning and Numeracy

● Make a bar chart or pictogram of how the children travel to nursery/school each day. Help the children to read the results using counting skills. Sing the question 'How did you travel to school today?' to the tune of 'Here we go round the mulberry bush'. All the children who came on foot can reply: 'We walked to school this morning.' (N2, 6)

● Provide a selection of plastic animals and minibeasts for the children to sort according to the number of legs they have or how they move, that is run, crawl, jump, fly. (N5, 6)

Knowledge and Understanding of the World

● Help the children to discover more about where they live (see activity opposite). (K9, 10)

● Invite them to draw a simple map of their journey home. (K9, 10)

Physical Development

● Make a diagram or plan of the equipment in the room. Ask the children to estimate how many steps it will take to walk from the climbing frame to the door. Use picture cards to plan a route round the room. Introduce directions and positional language - left, right, under, behind and so on. (PD1, 2, 3, 4)

● Play the follow-my-leader game (see activity opposite). (PD2, 4)

● Put a thin layer of dry sand or a mixture of cornflour and water in a shallow tray. Ask the children to take their finger for a journey to make a long, winding road. Can they follow instructions about which directions to take? (PD2, 8)

Creative Development

- Roll out some lining paper on the floor and ask the children to go on a paint walk. Hold the child's hand as they step in the tray of paint and walk along the paper. Have a bowl of water ready at the end to wash the shoes. Try this with shoes on and off to make a variety of footprints. Cut out the prints and make trails on the floor for the children to follow. (C3)
- Go on a listening walk around the room or outside. Help the children to notice the different sounds around them. Try recording the sounds and listening back to them. Can the children find ways of reproducing the sounds using their voices, body sounds or percussion? (C1, 4)

Activity: I live at ...

Learning opportunity: Looking at maps and observing local environment.

Early Learning Goal: Knowledge and Understanding of the World. Children will be able to observe, find out about and identify features in the place they live and the natural world. They will find out about their environment, and talk about those features they like and dislike.

Resources: Enlarged photocopied map of local area; blown-up photographs of local buildings and features, for example nursery/school, park, shops, church; string; coloured stickers; paper; felt pens.

Organisation: Small group.

Key vocabulary: Live, map, local, address, road, street, name of your local town, nearest, furthest.

What to do: Display the map on a board so that all the children can see. Talk about each of the photographs and stick them around the edge of the map, linking them with string.

Ask children to find their homes on the map and mark them with coloured stickers. Who lives furthest away? How do the children come to school?

Help the children to complete the sentence 'I live at...'. Talk about why it is important to remember their address. Help them to scribe their addresses and compile into a group address book.

Can the children draw pictures of their homes to display with the map? What do they like or dislike about where they live?

Activity: Follow me to school

Learning opportunity: Listening and responding as a group in a follow-my-leader game.

Early Learning Goal: Physical Development. Children will be able to move with confidence, imagination and in safety. They will move with control and coordination. They will show awareness of space, of themselves and of others.

Resources: A copy of the song 'I went to school one morning and I walked like this' from This Little Puffin; tambourine; bells.

Organisation: Whole group.

Key vocabulary: This will depend on the verses used and on other ideas of how to move suggested by the children.

What to do: Sitting in a circle on the floor, sing the song with the children and ask for volunteers to move around making up appropriate actions for each verse. Can they think of other ways of moving around and getting to school? Ask the children to stand in a long line and follow you around the room copying the different ways of moving. Encourage some of the children to take a turn at being the leader and choosing how to move. Extend the game by introducing music signals. Ask the children to move round in a circle. When they hear one beat on the tambourine, they must turn round and walk in the opposite direction. Two beats - change speed, three beats - change level, that is on tip-toe or close to the floor. What could they do when they hear the bells?

Display

Divide a board in half labelled 'left' and 'right'. Cut out and mount some of the foot paintings. Can the children sort them into left and right prints?

Display the book 'Journeys the children have made on foot' and add to it as the topic continues. Begin a display of books used during the week and ask children to find other books for each week of the theme.

Week 2
By road

Personal, Social and Emotional Development

● Talk about the different reasons for making journeys by road, such as going to nursery/school, shopping, doctors, holidays, visiting friends and relatives. As a group, cut out and paint a big car shape and add labels including all the children's reasons. Do they enjoy all of these journeys? (PS4, 8)

● During circle time, talk about keeping safe on roads (see activity opposite). (PS5, 7, 10, 11)

Communication, Language and Literacy

● On a large sheet of paper draw the outline of a double-decker bus with four windows on each level. Ask children to draw a different face in each window. Help them to make up stories explaining the reason why each passenger is making this bus journey. Scribe stories into a group book. (L1, 7, 13, 16)

● Take a small group of children to visit a local travel agency. Set up the role-play area as a travel agency. Make tickets and booking forms. Provide a desk, telephones, an old computer keyboard and screen. Display posters and brochures from travel agencies. Encourage children to take turns in booking a holiday. Where would they like to visit? How will they travel there? (L2, 7, 17)

Problem Solving, Reasoning and Numeracy

● Make simple number plates for all the sit-and-ride toys. Help each child to create a personalised number plate (see activity opposite). (N1, 3)

● Look at pictures of road signs and discuss the shapes used. Tell the children what some of the signs mean. Ask them to choose a shape and design a road sign to use in the road layout (see Physical Development). (N11, 12)

● Organise a traffic survey. Make a list of road vehicles. Ask a small group of children to spend five minutes watching the traffic and mark what they see on the list. Count and compare the results. (N1, 2, 5)

Knowledge and Understanding of the World

● Show children a selection of toy vehicles. Help them to make model vehicles out of a variety of construction toys. Organise a model car show when children can talk about how they built each model. How easy was it to put together? Do the wheels rotate smoothly? How fast can they travel? (K3, 4, 5)

● Use a variety of junk materials such as boxes, tubes, bottle tops and corks to make 3-d models of road vehicles. Show them how to construct simple axles using thin dowelling and cotton reels. Use a word processor to make name labels for each model vehicle. (K5, 6)

Physical Development

● Set out a road layout or circuit with road signs, crossings, and obstacles for children to move round on sit-and-ride vehicles. Ask children to complete a set number of laps. Let them take turns using a simple stop/go sign (red/green circles). (PD1, 2, 3, 4)

● Play the traffic lights game with colours. Green - move forward, amber - jump up and down on the spot, red - stop still like a statue! Try using three percussion sounds instead of colours, such as claves, maracas, bells. (PD2)

Creative Development

● Paint with toy vehicles. Let children choose a plastic car or lorry and drive it through the paint in a shallow tray and then onto long strips of black paper. Add white lines to the paper roads. Talk about the patterns and different treads on the tyres. (C2, 3)

● Enjoy adding percussion and vocal sound effects to the story of 'The Big Blue Jeep and the Little White Trike' from Three Tapping Teddies (see Resources). (C2, 4)

Activity: Keeping safe on the road

Learning opportunity: Discussing how to keep safe on the pavement and in the car.

Early Learning Goal: Personal, Social and Emotional Development. Children will have a developing awareness of their own needs, views and feelings and be sensitive to the needs, views and feelings of others. They will consider the consequences of their words and actions for themselves and others.

Resources: Visitor - school crossing patrol officer or road safety officer; contact RoSPA (Royal Society for the Prevention of Accidents) for a variety of resources; zebra or pelican crossing.

Organisation: Whole group.

Key vocabulary: Safe, wait, look, listen, traffic lights, seat belt.

What to do: Talk about how important it is to keep safe on the road. Ask the children for their ideas about how to keep themselves safe. How many of them can help to fasten their seat belt in the car? Why is it important to wear a seat belt? Introduce the visitor (if available). Encourage the children to listen attentively and respond appropriately.

Set up a crossing in the room using borrowed or handmade resources and add to the road layout (see Physical Development). Talk about how the crossings work. What do the different coloured lights and images indicate? Let the children role play drivers and pedestrians. Invite the children to work in pairs, and help each other to cross the road safely. Did they remember to stop, look and listen? Remind the children to always hold an adult's hand when they cross the road. Play 'Trust' by blindfolding one child in the pair. Use sounds to help them know when to cross the road.

Activity: Number plates

Learning opportunity: Looking at number plates and designing personalised plates for themselves.

Early Learning Goal: Problem Solving, Reasoning and Numeracy. Children should recognise numerals one to nine.

Resources: A variety of sit-and-ride toys sporting a prepared set of number plates; a matching set of laminated plates; pre-cut rectangles of card; access to a word processor and printer; sheet of numbers and letters; glue.

Organisation: Small group.

Key vocabulary: Numbers one to nine, number plate, match, personalised, registration.

What to do: Take the children outside and show them some number plates on cars. Look at pictures of cars and discuss the purpose of the plates. How many numbers

and letters are there on each plate? Do they know the registration of their car?

Help the children to attach the number plates to the sit-and-ride toys. Invite them to play a matching game with the extra set of plates. Can they role play a traffic police officer and write down the number plates of the cars that pass them?

Ask the children to design their own personalised number plate using an abbreviation of their name and age, such as SAM 3, or HAN 4. Help the children to make the plates using a word processor or pre-printed numbers.

Explain that they could play simple travel games using number plates when on journeys with their parents. Can they see all the numbers from nought to nine? Who will be first to spot an X?

Display
Involve the children in creating a display using the 3-d junk models and construction models made during the week. Place them on a road layout on a table and add the printed name cards. Decorate the background with the tyre and tread paintings.

Week 3
By rail track or trail

Personal, Social and Emotional Development

- Play the circle train game. Each child in the circle repeats the phrase 'We're going on a train to visit ...' and has to choose in turn to add a person/ place/time/reason. (PS1, 2, 8)
- Discuss travelling on underground or tube trains and through dark tunnels. How does it feel to travel at night? (PS4, 5)
- Read *Sloth's Shoes* by Jeanne Willis (Red Fox). Talk about being late for things. (PS3, 4, 10)

Communication, Language and Literacy

- Make a train station in the role-play area, with tickets, timetables, signs showing departures and arrivals, lost property office. Organise a ticket office for children to buy and sell tickets. Provide dressing-up clothes and props for the train driver and guard. Use a row of chairs for the train carriage. (L1, 2, 5, 7)
- Give each child as many pre-cut train carriages as there are letters in their name. Help them to find an engine with their initial letter written on. Show them how to arrange the name trains by adding subsequent letters to the carriages. Allow them to write independently, or copy. Thread the carriages together and display them. (L9, 10)

Problem Solving, Reasoning and Numeracy

- Look at some train timetables. Why do we need them? Use a large model clock to introduce o'clock times to the children. Add a time dimension to the role-play train station with a notice saying 'The train will leave at 10 o'clock this morning'. If each journey lasts for one hour, help the children to work out some timetables. (N1, 4, 7)
- Use a stop watch to time the children making simple journeys around the room, such as from the table to the door. (N1, 2, 6)
- Give each child a cut-out train shape with no wheels. Play a game in which the children take it in turns to roll a die and collect the corresponding number of wheels to add to their train. (N2, 3)

Knowledge and Understanding of the World

- Go outside and look for tracks and trails made by people and animals (see activity opposite). (K2, 3)
- Look at trains, then and now. Use non-fiction books and find out about how different trains work. Use a writing frame to help the children consolidate these ideas: then - steam trains (like Thomas the Tank Engine!); now - electric trains. Extend this to other journeys: then - horse and cart; now - car, plane and so on. (K2, 4, 8)

Physical Development

- Use white chalk to draw parallel tracks on the ground. Choose two or three children to be engines and have a small group of children as their train by holding onto each other. Can they chug carefully along the tracks like trains? (PD1, 2, 4)
- Lay a trail of animal prints around the room. Invite the children to move like a variety of animals along the trail. Provide tunnels and hoops to crawl through, and balance beams to make the journey more challenging. Cover the tunnels with old curtains or sheets to make them dark. Can the children freeze when they hear a chosen sound such as a bell or a shaken maraca? (PD1, 3, 7)

Creative Development

- Make some salt dough with the children. Cut out train shapes. Paint them in bright colours and add trucks, numbers and so on. (C2)
- Explore fast and slow using train rhythms and percussion instruments (see activity opposite). (C2, 4, 5)
- Print train tracks using the edges of strips of corrugated cardboard. Help children to print trains on the tracks using a variety of plastic bricks and cotton reels. Invite the children to help mount their work ready for display. (C3, 5)

Activity: Snail trails

Learning opportunity: Examining tracks and trails made by different creatures.

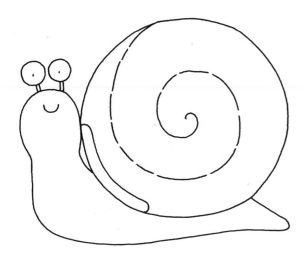

Early Learning Goal: Knowledge and Understanding of the World. Children will be able to find out about and identify some features of living things, objects and events they observe. They will look closely at similarities, differences, patterns and change.

Resources: Outside area or garden; containers; magnifying glasses.

Organisation: Small group.

Key vocabulary: Tracks, trails, prints, snails, other animals.

What to do: Go outside early in the morning and look on the ground for any footprints or tracks. Explain to the children what you are looking for. If it has rained recently they may see tracks made by pushchairs or their own footprints. If it is dry, ask the children to step into a tray of water and make some prints.

If possible, point out prints or tracks made by other creatures. Encourage the children to look closely for snails on the plants. Can they see the glistening trails left by the snails? Put some snails in a container and take them carefully inside. Use magnifying glasses to examine them as they move. Place two snails on a piece of paper and watch them race. Look at the silvery trails they leave behind.

Use PVA glue and glitter to make winding snail trails on black paper.

Don't forget to return the snails safely to their natural habitat!

Activity: Train rhythms

Learning opportunity: Experimenting with speed/tempo and exploring the rhythmic sound of trains.

Early Learning Goal: Creative Development. Children will be able to recognise and explore how sounds can be changed, sing simple songs, recognise repeated sounds and sound patterns and match movements to music.

Resources: Prepared cards with fast/slow and symbols (see illustration); percussion instruments.

Organisation: Whole group.

Key vocabulary: Listen, fast, slow, tempo, rhythm.

What to do: Ask all the children to stand in a circle and walk round in time to a steady beat played on a drum or claves. When the tempo changes, that is the beat speeds up or slows down, encourage the children to match it.

Introduce the cards showing the words and symbols. Practise singing 'The wheels on the bus/train' either 'fast' or 'slow'. Invite the children to take turns at conducting the singing using the cards.

Teach the children this train rhythm:

```
1       2        3    4
Dum   dee-dee dum        dee-dee
```

Then try this one:
```
1        2    3       4
Diddle-ee-dee      diddle-ee-dee
```

Can they keep the rhythm going as they move around the circle? Try slowing down and speeding up. Add percussion instruments for sound effects of doors opening and closing, people talking, whistles blowing and so on.

Ask some of the children to sing the song while the others keep the rhythm going.

Display

Cut round some of the printed tracks and make a track layout for the dough models and name trains.

Display some photographs of different animals and their tracks. Mount and display the snail trails. Ask the children to draw or potato print some simple animal prints in between the artwork.

Week 4
On or under water

Personal, Social and Emotional Development

● Make a collection of picture books about boats. Talk about going on a boat trip or cruise. Emphasise the importance of behaving sensibly by water. Encourage children to realise that they have an important part to play in keeping themselves safe. (PS9, 10)

● Talk about people who work at sea such as fishermen, lifeboat men and lighthouse keepers. Write a group letter to the RNLI (see 'Resources') to say thank-you for the work they do. (PS5, 7, 8)

Communication, Language and Literacy

● Read *Mr Gumpy's Outing* by John Burningham. Put together a story bag containing toys of all the characters and a plastic boat. At the water tray ask children to take turns to carefully put a toy in the boat until it capsizes. Encourage children to draw pictures to illustrate the story. (L4, 13)

● Introduce the idea of keeping a daily diary about a journey. As a group, write an imaginary journal about a long voyage on a boat. (L1, 4, 7)

● Make a collection of watery words (see activity opposite). (L5, 9, 12)

Problem Solving, Reasoning and Numeracy

● Colour the water in the water tray and provide plenty of transparent water toys, including tubing, plastic bottles, funnels and so on. Encourage the use of a variety of mathematical language as the children play. Which is the longest tube? Which container holds the most water? (N4, 9)

● Go on a shape or number journey inside or outside. Sing 'We're going on a shape walk, a shape walk, a shape walk. We're going on a shape walk, to see what we can see' (Tune: 'Poor Jenny is a-weeping'). Help the children to record the shapes and/or numbers they see. (N1, 2, 11, 12)

Knowledge and Understanding of the World

● Introduce the words 'float' and 'sink' (see activity opposite). (K4)

● Provide a selection of different paper such as newspaper, sugar paper, tissue paper, cardboard. Help the children to make folded paper boats.

Which paper boat keeps afloat the longest? Blow through straws to make the boats move on the water. (K1, 4, 5)

Physical Development

● Ask the children to choose a partner and sit opposite each other to make a boat shape. Sing 'Row, row, row the boat' while rowing. Alternatively, provide a selection of large cardboard boxes to use as boats. Shallow fruit boxes are ideal. Oars can be improvised from long cardboard tubes. (PD2, 4, 6)

● Play 'Treasure islands'. Use mats as islands or use chalk to draw island shapes. Choose two children to be the hungry sharks. Invite the rest of the children to row around the islands avoiding the sharks. On a chosen signal, such as a shaken tambourine, all the boats must find refuge on an island before the sharks strike. Any children who are caught can join the sharks. Encourage the children to listen carefully to the instructions and to take care not to ollide into each other. (PD1, 2, 4)

Creative Development

● Make simple sailing boats or yachts using a large triangle of paper. Fold up the base of the shape to make the boat. Ask the children to name their boat and design a pattern on the sail. (C3)

● Mix together blue paint and washing-up liquid to make bubble prints. Use this to create a watery background and stick cut-out fishes, sea creatures and real shells in the foreground. Help the children to frame their underwater pictures with shiny card. (C2)

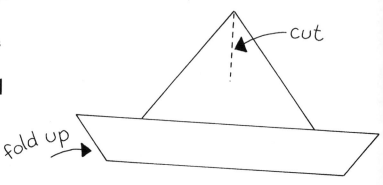

● Talk about what they might see on an undersea journey - fish, mermaids, sharks, octopus, wrecks, buried treasure and so on. Listen to some watery music such as 'La Mer' by Debussy, 'Orinoco Flow' by Enya or 'Under the sea' from The Little Mermaid (Disney). Work with the children to improvise a drama about the undersea world. Use a camcorder to film the story. (C1, 2, 5)

Activity: Watery words

Learning opportunity: Using descriptive words and sounds to build up a picture of the word 'water'.

Early Learning Goal: Communication, Language and Literacy. Children will be able to explore and experiment with sounds, words and texts. They will extend their vocabulary, exploring the meaning and sounds of new words. They will hear and say initial sounds in words.

Resources: Large piece of card; raindrop shapes cut from silver paper; string; large sealed plastic bottle with a small amount of coloured water inside; percussion instruments.

Organisation: Whole group.

Key vocabulary: Water, drop, drip, splash, puddle, gush, wet.

What to do: Explain to the children that you are going to think about watery words. In the middle of a large piece of card write the word 'water'. Cut the card into the shape of a cloud. Notice the initial sound 'w'. Encourage children to think of other words that begin with 'w'.

Ask children to help you make a list of words that describe water or the sound it makes. Write these out and stick them onto the silver raindrops. Arrange them around the word 'water' and hang them from the cloud with string.

Show children the bottle of water and let some try turning it upside down to hear the sound. Let them experiment and make different sounds. Now can they think of some more watery words to add to the cloud?

Help children to make vocal or body sounds that sound like water. Which instruments could they use? Maracas, home-made shakers and rainsticks are particularly effective. Go round the group and ask each child to say a word or make a sound to create a watery sound collage or journey.

Activity: Boats should float

Learning opportunity: Exploring aspects of floating and sinking.

Early Learning Goal: Knowledge and Understanding of the World. Children will be able to investigate objects and materials by using all of their senses as appropriate. They will ask questions about why things happen and how things work.

Resources: A deep, clear plastic or glass bowl; selection of items to test: corks, nuts, shells, wood, paper, marble, plastic spoon, apple, pebble, metal key and so on; piece of card divided into two columns headed 'float' and 'sink'.

Organisation: Small group of children at a table.

Key vocabulary: Float, sink, on, under, predict.

What to do: Introduce the terms 'float' (on the water) and 'sink' (under the water) by demonstrating with a plastic boat. Show them that boats will float unless they fill up with water!

Explain they are going to investigate whether different materials float or sink. Encourage children to predict whether an item will float or sink before testing it. Put all the items they think will float in one group, and the things they think will sink in another. Ask children to test their predictions. Were they right? Which results surprise them? What happens to the plastic spoon? Ask them to record their results on the chart. Help children to draw and label items in the correct columns. Ask them to share their discoveries with the whole group.

Display

Use toys from the story bag and the children's drawings to make a display of Mr Gumpy's Outing. Display the children's underwater bubble pictures and folded boats. Hang up the watery words cloud. Make a display in the water tray of all the boats the children have made and played with during the week.

Week 5
Through the air

Personal, Social and Emotional Development

- At circle time, invite adults to come in and talk to children about journeys they have made. (PS3, 7)
- Make a collection of postcards and photographs from different countries. Display them on a board with a map of the world. Talk about how it feels to receive a letter or postcard. Help children to make postcards to send to friends or parents. Encourage them to draw a design or stick a picture on one side and write a simple message and address on the other. Walk to the nearest postbox and post them. (PS4, 6, 12)

Communication, Language and Literacy

- Introduce passports and help children to make their own (see activity opposite). (L17, 18, 19)
- Talk with children about packing a suitcase to fly on holiday to another country. Play 'When I pack to go away I need...' with each child adding a new item. Help them to think about how the contents would change according to the climate. (L1, 3, 8)
- Read *Whatever Next?* by Jill Murphy (Macmillan Children's Books). Make a collection of props from the story such as a colander, wellies, teddy, chocolate biscuits, apple, jar of honey, toy owl. Put all of these in a large cardboard box and encourage the children to enjoy retelling and acting out the story. (L4, 7, 13)

Problem Solving, Reasoning and Numeracy

- Make a number frieze with a flying theme (see activity opposite). (N2, 3)
- Select four different-sized suitcases and ask the children to sort them according to size. Encourage use of lots of mathematical language. Fill them with a variety of surprise items and sort them according to weight. Make sure that the smallest case is the heaviest! Provide a set of bathroom scales so that children can actually weigh the cases. Use these in the airport role-play area as part of the check-in desk. (N9, 11)

Knowledge and Understanding of the World

- Read *Honk! Honk!* by Mick Manning (Kingfisher). Look at birds in flight and on the ground. How do they move? Talk about the journeys that migrating birds make to warm countries during the winter. Look at a map or globe to see how far they travel. (K2, 4)
- Read *Percy's Bumpy Ride* by Nick Butterworth (Picture Lions). Invite children to draw a design for a flying machine. Use soft wood, nails, bottle tops, strips of card to construct magnificent flying machines. (K4, 5, 6)

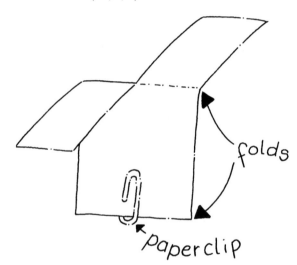

- Help the children to fold paper into simple planes. Make spinning helicopters with paper and paper clips (see diagram) and drop them from the top of the climbing frame. Which design flies the fastest or furthest? (K1, 4, 5)

Physical Development

- Give the children a small suitcase and a list of things to pack for themselves or teddy. Help them to find all the things. Can they fit them all into the case? Help them to fold the clothes neatly. (PD5, 7)
- Help children to partially inflate about ten balloons. Enjoy playing with them on the parachute (or improvise by using a sari cut in half and sewn into a square). Sing:
The balloons are floating up and down,
Up and down, up and down.
The balloons are floating up and down,
Watch them flying.
(Tune: 'London Bridge is falling down') (PD2, 7)

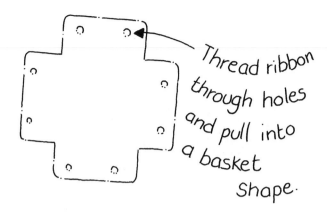

Thread ribbon through holes and pull into a basket shape.

Creative Development

- Transform the role-play area into an airport with baggage check-in, customs, and airport shop. Help children to write luggage labels and tickets. Display clocks showing the time in different countries. Arrange pairs of chairs in a row for the cabin and provide a trolley with refreshments for flight attendants to distribute. Paint an instrument panel for the pilot using fluorescent paints on black paper. Invite children to dress up and enjoy role playing the crew and passengers. (C5)
- Make papier maché hot-air balloons and hang small card baskets (see diagram) under them. (C2)

Activity: Don't forget your passport!

Learning opportunity: Drawing and writing about themselves to make passports.

Early Learning Goal: Communication, Language and Literacy. Children should attempt writing for various purposes, using features of different forms such as lists, stories and instructions. They should write their own names, labels and captions.

Resources: Paper folded into passport-sized book; pencils; felt pens; stamps and printing ink.

Organisation: Small group.

Key vocabulary: Passport, identification, photograph.

What to do: Show children your own passport. Explain that everyone has to take their passport with them when travelling on a journey to another country.

Help children make a list of what is needed in a passport such as a photograph, date of birth and signature. Ask children to draw small colour self-portraits for their passports. Provide mirrors so they can observe hair and eye colour accurately. Do they know their dates of birth? Talk about the difference between writing their

name and their signature. Show them some examples. Invite children to write their signature in their passports. Encourage children to design a front cover for their passports. Can they include the name of the school in the design?

Let children enjoy using their passports in role play at the airport. The customs officer must stamp the passport before they board the plane!

Activity: Flying high

Learning opportunity: Using a counting rhyme to count, recognise and match numbers.

Early Learning Goal: Problem Solving, Reasoning and Numeracy. Children should count reliably up to ten everyday objects. They will recognise numerals one to nine.

Resources: Pre-cut numbers and shapes for picture; paints; selection of collage materials; glue.

Organisation: Whole group introduction, small group for artwork.

Key vocabulary: Words and numerals one to six.

What to do: Use carpet or circle time to enjoy learning this number rhyme:

One plane flying so high
Two birds swooping through the sky
Three insects buzzing around
Four kites falling to the ground
Five rockets zooming away
Six stars shining at the end of the day.

Help the correct number of children to say each line and add appropriate actions.

In small groups, make the different items for the picture. Invite children to select suitable colours and collage materials. Use the word processor to print the words of the rhyme to add to the display.

Display

Mount the children's designs for magnificent flying machines and display their 3-d models. Suspend the hot-air balloons from the ceiling at different levels. The children can add small world play people and animals to the baskets. Invite them to draw pictures or maps of what they might see from the air.

Week 6
Anywhere and everywhere

Personal, Social and Emotional Development
- Introduce a special 'Journey Bear' to the group. Invite children to take it in turns to take the bear on holiday or an outing. Ask them to bring back a photograph of 'Journey Bear in...'. Make a photo album of the bear's travels. (PS8, 13)
- Talk about the outing which will take place this week. What will children need to bring with them? How are they going to travel? What do they think they will see on the way there? Discuss how to behave in new places. (PS5, 9)

Communication, Language and Literacy
- Prepare cards showing different vehicles (words and pictures). As you tell a story, children listen for their vehicle, holding up the card and making an appropriate sound or action whenever it is mentioned. Invite children to make up a story for the others to listen to. (L2, 4, 12)
- Invite children to think about a journey they are going to make. Play a game using question words: Where/why/when are you going? How are you getting there? What will you do there? Print the question words on five cards and place them face down. Take turns to choose a question. (L8, 14)

Problem Solving, Reasoning and Numeracy
- Help children to sort a selection of toy vehicles according to different criteria, such as number of wheels, wings, colours, propellers, and so on. (N1, 2)
- Introduce ordinal numbers. Make a display of five different vehicles labelled first to fifth. Ask children to describe the second, the fourth and so on. Which vehicle is behind the bus? (N1, 3, 12)

Knowledge and Understanding of the World
- Use a map to show children the route you will take on your outing. Talk about what they might see on the way there. Draw a simplified route on paper for children to follow with their fingers or pencils. (K9)
- Use cardboard shapes, paper fasteners, art straws, string and sticky tape to make 2-d models of moving machines. Encourage the children to use their imaginations and make up names for their fantasy machines. (K5, 6)

- Choose a country and invite the group and parents to 'Come on a day trip to France or Spain or China...'. Encourage children to dress up in suitable costumes, try new food, listen to music and stories, play games, learn about special customs, and say a few simple words related to the choice of country. If there is a child from another country in the group already, this can be a good starting point. (K11)

Physical Development
- Play the 'Journeys game' (see activity opposite). (PD1, 2, 4)
- Play team travel relay. Help children into two teams and number them one, two, three and so on. Ask both number ones to skip down the room and back, then both number twos to walk backwards, and so on. (PD2, 4)

Creative Development
- Practise the 'Outing song':
  We're going to visit a ... today.
  There's lots of things to do and play.
  What do you think we'll see on the way (today).
  ... insert some of children's ideas
  (Tune: 'I went to visit a farm one day') (C4)
- Ask children to close their eyes and come with you for a ride on a magic carpet (see activity opposite). (C1, 5)

Activity: The journeys game

Learning opportunity: Listening to instructions and moving around the room collaboratively in a game.

Early Learning Goal: Physical Development. Children will be able to move with confidence, imagination and safety. They will move with control and coordination. They will show awareness of space, of themselves and others.

Resources: None.

Organisation: Whole group in a large space.
Key vocabulary: Flying, pedalling, galloping, driving, floating and so on.

What to do: This is a variation on the game 'Beans'. Each instruction is a 'vehicle' which initiates an action from the children. When playing for the first time just use three or four different vehicles. Add more ideas each time you play. Ask children if they can think of new ideas.

Here are some to get you started:
car - drive around pretending to use a steering wheel
horse - gallop
aeroplane - fly around with arms extended
hot-air balloon - hold both hands up high to make a balloon shape and glide
skates - slide around floor
bicycle - lie on floor and cycle legs in air
wheelbarrow - in pairs, one child holds legs of other who walks on hands

Activity: On a magic carpet

Learning opportunity: Listening and responding as a group in an imaginative role-play context.

Early Learning Goal: Creative Development. Children will be able to respond in a variety of ways to what they see, hear, smell, touch and feel. They will use their imagination in art and design, music, dance, imaginative and role play and stories.

Resources: Large mat or carpet to sit on.

Organisation: Small group.

Key vocabulary: Pretend, listen, imagine, far away, nearby, down, below, souvenir.

What to do: Start with the children sitting comfortably on the carpet. Tell them you are going to pretend that

this carpet is a magic one that will fly them anywhere they wish. Ask if you can have the first wish.

Ask all the children to shut their eyes and listen as you tell them about the journey. Describe in detail everything you pass on the way. When you arrive, invite them to imagine that they are walking around. What can they see, hear, smell and touch? Can they choose one thing to bring back with them to show the others - a souvenir?

These are a few places you might visit:

Seaside: past houses, fields, roads, traffic jams; feel it getting warmer; paddle in the sea; build sandcastles; choose a shell to bring back.

North Pole: past land and sea, islands; feel it getting colder; climb on the icebergs; hide from a polar bear; bring back a stone.

Bedroom: past school playground, houses, shops; up the stairs; see your toys; choose one special toy to bring back. When you have been on a few journeys you can invite children to have a go at wishing and describing what they can see.

Display
Illustrate your 'Come on a day trip to ....' with pictures of the chosen country, and photographs from the day itself. Let children help you compose suitable captions for them. Make a display of the models of moving machines and help children to use IT to produce labels.

Bringing It All Together

The outing

Before starting the Journeys topic, make some initial plans for the outing including booking any transport required. When choosing a suitable place to visit try contacting your local tourist information office for advice. Local farm centres, parks, museums and steam train stations usually offer appropriate activities for young children. Check details with your choice of destination about availability, cost, picnic area, toilet facilities, covered area for wet weather, shop and so on. Ask for a brochure to show the children and their parents.

Introducing the outing

At the start of the topic, inform parents about the outing and invite them to come along. Make it clear whether younger siblings are allowed to come or not.

Nearer the time display the brochure and invite the children to help make posters including vital information about where and when they are going, cost, and what they will need to bring with them.

Explain to the children that in a few days time they are going to go on the outing. Talk about how to behave when travelling in a bus, coach or train. Emphasise the importance of keeping safe and the need to listen to the adults with them. If visiting a farm, talk to the children about hygiene and the need to wash their hands after touching or feeding any of the animals.

Preparations

Involve the children in deciding what food they should bring in their packed lunch. Provide an outline of a lunch box and ask them to draw a picture of what they would like to eat to show their parents. What is the most popular sandwich filling? Is it a good idea to bring lots of chocolate biscuits on a hot day? Encourage them to think about healthy food.

Other useful items to take include a supply of spare clothes, baby wipes, bucket in case of travel sickness, and a first aid kit.

The weather

Talk about how the weather may affect the outing. What will the children need to bring with them in case it rains? Why is it important to wear a sunhat or sun cream in the hot sunshine?

On the journey

Make sure all the adults and children know where they are going and which adult is responsible for each child. Encourage the children to join in with the 'Outing song' (see Week 6: Creative Development) and other appropriate travel songs such as 'The wheels on the bus' and 'Old Macdonald had a farm'.

Play some games on the way: 'I went on a journey and saw a ...'. Invite one child to start the game with an idea. The following child must remember the items already on the list before adding their own. Encourage recognition of initial sounds by playing a game of 'I spy' referring to things seen on the journey or while on the outing.

Invite one of the parents to record key moments of the outing on a video camera, and another to take photographs for compiling into a big book to commemorate the special day.

Follow-up activities

Make a book of observational drawings and writing about the outing entitled 'Our Journey to...'. Ask children to paint a favourite thing they saw or did. Frame their work and hold an exhibition to invite parents and friends to view. Help the children to compile a catalogue of paintings on show.

Home alternative

If for any reason organising an outing is not possible, try holding a sponsored circuit or 'journey' using all the climbing and balancing equipment as an obstacle course. Ask children to collect sponsors for how many circuits they can complete. Provide lots of drinks for the children to serve each other refreshments. Invite parents to come and cheer them on and join in a group picnic at the end of their exertions! Use the money collected to give to a local charity or buy a special new piece of equipment for the children.

Resources

Resources to collect
- A local map of the area.
- Selection of plastic animals and minibeasts.
- Travel brochures and posters.
- Pictures of car number plates and road signs.
- Train timetables.
- A stopwatch.
- Music for undersea journey such as 'La Mer' by Debussy.
- Postcards and photographs from around the world.
- A globe.
- Several different-sized suitcases.
- Balloons.

Everyday resources
- Bottle lids, corks, large and small boxes for modelling, cardboard and plastic tubes.
- Papers and cards of different weights, colours and textures, for example sugar, corrugated card, lining paper, silver and shiny papers.
- Dry powder paints for mixing and mixed paints for covering large areas and printing.
- Different sized paint brushes from household brushes and rollers to thin brushes for delicate work, and a variety of paint mixing containers.
- A variety of drawing and colouring pencils, crayons, chalks, pastels, and felt pens.
- Soft wood, hammers, nails, lolly sticks, and bottle lids for woodwork modelling.
- Percussion instruments.

Stories
- *Alfie's Feet* by Shirley Hughes (Red Fox).
- *Mr Gumpy's Outing* by John Burningham (Red Fox).
- *Whatever Next?* by Jill Murphy (Macmillan Children's Books).
- *Honk! Honk!* by Mick Manning (Kingfisher).
- *Percy's Bumpy Ride* by Nick Butterworth (Picture Lions).
- *Sailor Bear* by Martin Waddell (Walker).
- *My Days Out* by Nick Sharratt (OUP).
- *Paddington Bear Stories* by Michael Bond (Collins).
- *The Journey Home from Grandpa's* by Jemima Lumley (Barefoot Books).
- *The Train Ride* by June Crebbin (Walker).
- *Frog and the Wide World* by Max Velthuijs (Andersen).
- *Through the Magic Mirror* by Anthony Browne (Walker).
- *Sloth's Shoes* by Jeanne Willis (Red Fox).
- *The Treasure Hunt* by Nick Butterworth (Picture Lions).
- *The School Trip* by Nick Butterworth (Hodder).

Non-Fiction
- *First Picture Atlas* (Kingfisher).
- *Train Journey (follow the map)* by Deborah Chancellor (Franklin Watts).
- *Incredible Flying Machines* by Christopher Maynard (Dorling Kindersley).
- *Travelling in Grandma's Day* by Faye Gardner (Evans).
- *Look out on the road* by Paul Humphrey/Red Rainbows Safety series (Evans).
- *Children from Australia to Zimbabwe: A photographic Journey Around the World* by Maya Ajmera (Shakli for Children).

Songs and rhymes
- *This Little Puffin* by Elizabeth Matterson (Puffin).
- *We're Going on a Bear Hunt* by Michael Rosen (Walker).
- *Out and About* by Shirley Hughes (Walker).
- *Three Tapping Teddies: Musical stories and charts for the very young* by Kaye Umansky (A & C Black).

Books for planning
- *The Early Years Foundation Stage; Setting the Standards for Learning, Development and Care for Children From Birth to Five* (Department for Children, Schools and Families).

Useful addresses
- RoSPA (Royal Society for the Prevention of Accidents), Edgbaston Park, 353 Bristol Road, Birmingham B5 7ST. Tel: 0121 248 2134.
- RNLI (Royal National Lifeboat Insititute), West Quay Road, Poole, Dorset BH15 1HZ. Tel: 0845 122 6999

Collecting Evidence of Children's Learning

Monitoring children's development is an important task. Keeping a record of children's achievements, interests and learning styles will help you to see progress and will draw attention to those who are having difficulties for some reason. If a child needs additional professional help, such as speech therapy, your records will provide valuable evidence.

Records should be the result of collaboration between group leaders, parents and carers. Parents should be made aware of your record keeping policies when their child joins your group. Show them the type of records you are keeping and make sure they understand that they have an opportunity to contribute. As a general rule, your records should form an open document. Any parent should have access to records relating to his or her child. Take regular opportunities to talk to parents about children's progress. If you have formal discussions regarding children about whom you have particular concerns, a dated record of the main points should be kept.

Keeping it manageable

Records should be helpful in informing group leaders, adult helpers and parents and always be for the benefit of the child. The golden rule is to make them simple, manageable and useful.

Observations will basically fall into three categories:

- **Spontaneous records:** Sometimes you will want to make a note of observations as they happen, for example, a child is heard counting cars accurately during a play activity, or is seen to play collaboratively for the first time.

- **Planned observations:** Sometimes you will plan to make observations of children's developing skills in their everyday activities. Using the learning opportunity identified for an activity will help you to make appropriate judgements about children's capabilities and to record them systematically.

To collect information:
- talk to children about their activities and listen to their responses;
- listen to children talking to each other;
- observe children's work such as early writing, drawings, paintings and 3D models. (Keeping photocopies or photographs is useful.)

Sometimes you may wish to set up 'one off' activities for the purposes of monitoring development. Some pre-school groups, for example, ask children to make a drawing of themselves at the beginning of each term to record their progressing skills in both co-ordination and observation. Do not attempt to make records after every activity!

- **Reflective observations:** It is useful to spend regular time reflecting on the children's progress. Aim to make some brief comments about each child every week.

Informing your planning

Collecting evidence about children's progress is time consuming and it is important that it is useful. When you are planning, use the information you have collected to help you to decide what learning opportunities you need to provide next for children. For example, a child who has poor pencil or brush control will benefit from more play with dough or construction toys to build the strength of hand muscles.

Example of recording chart

Name: Nina Giles		D.O.B. 22.2.04			Date of entry: 10.9.08	
Term	**Personal, Social and Emotional Development**	**Communication, Language and Literacy**	**Problem Solving, Reasoning and Numeracy**	**Knowledge and Understanding of the World**	**Physical Development**	**Creative Development**
ONE	Confident to try new activities. Talked about moving house and making new friends. 24.9.08 EMH	Enjoys listening to stories, especially *Mr Gumpy's Outing*. Can recognise and write name. 20.11.08 EMH	Counts to 12. Recognises numbers 1-9. Identifies shapes - circles, squares, triangles and rectangles. 6.11.08 BM	Eager to ask questions. Enjoyed building flying machines using wood. 17.10.08 PB	Lacks confidence when using large apparatus. Enjoyed making finger journeys in the cornflour. 28.9.08 AC	Loves using percussion to add sound effects. Enjoys role-play and drama, especially undersea story. 3.10.08 PB
TWO						
THREE						

Skills overview of six-week plan

Week	Topic Focus	Personal, Social and Emotional Development	Communication, Language and Literacy	Problem Solving, Reasoning and Numeracy	Knowledge and Understanding of the World	Physical Development	Creative Development
1	On foot	Awareness of safety; Care of others	Talking; Writing; Appreciating books	Counting; Sorting	Observing; Recording	Moving with control and imagination; Fine motor skills	Printing; Listening and making sounds
2	By road	Awarness of safety; Discussing feelings	Making up stories; Role-play	Counting; Matching shapes	Constructing; Using materials	Moving with control and coordination; Awareness of space	Painting; Making sounds
3	By rail, track or trail	Taking turns; Discussing feelings	Role-play; Recognising initial sounds	Measuring time; Counting	Investigating; Observing; Comparing	Moving safely with imagination; Using a range of equipment	Using malleable materials; Making sounds; Printing
4	On or under water	Awareness of safety; Saying thank-you	Writing; Exploring sounds; Retelling stories	Matching shapes; Using mathematical language; Estimating	Investigating; Talking; Using materials	Moving with imagination and awarness of space; Playing collaboratively	Using materials; Painting; Collage; Drama; Dance
5	Through the air	Listening; Discussing feelings	Writing for a purpose; Telling stories	Recognising numbers; Comparing; Measuring	Talking; Designing; Constructing	Fine motor skills; Working collaboratively	Role-play; Modelling
6	Anywhere and everywhere	Discussing feelings and behaviour; Collaborative planning	Talking; Writing questions	Sorting; Ordinal numbers	Recording; Constructing; Comparing	Playing collaboratively; Moving safely and confidently	Singing; Imaginative play; Printing; Listening

Home links

The theme of Journeys lends itself to useful links with children's homes and families. Through working together children and adults gain respect for each other and build comfortable and confident relationships.

Establishing partnerships

- Keep parents informed about the topic of Journeys, the themes for each week and details of the outing. By understanding the work of the group, parents will enjoy the involvement of contributing ideas, time and resources.
- Request parental permission before taking children out on a group journey on foot around the local area. Describe your planned route and explain the purposes of the walk. Additional parental help will be necessary for this activity to be carried out safely.
- Photocopy the parent's page for each child to take home.
- Invite parents and carers to accompany you on the outing.

Visiting enthusiasts

- Invite adults to come to the group and talk about interesting journeys they have made. Ensure that the visitors are well briefed so that children's attention can be sustained.

- If you have contacts with adults from other cultures invite them to visit the group and show the children pictures and share information about their country of origin.

Resource requests

- Ask parents to bring in any postcards or photographs of interesting places they have visited.
- Cotton reels, bottle tops and small boxes are useful for collage and construction activities.

The outing

- It is essential to have enough enthusiastic extra adults to accompany the children on the outing for safety reasons and to make the learning experience more valuable. Check that parents are happy to care for their own child and one or more other children if necessary.